The Ego Cleanse
Becoming Your Own Best Friend
By Randy Haveson, M.A.

ISBN: 978-0-9984138-0-8

First Edition

Printed in the United States

Dedication

With much gratitude, I dedicate this book to my parents, Sandy and Al Haveson, who taught me great life lessons from an early age. Also, to Dr. Charlie Nelson, your guidance and mentorship at the beginning of my sobriety helped shape me into the person I am today. To Phil W., Leon Kahane, and the woman at the 1-800-BE-SOBER hotline on May 16, 1984 at 1:00am who saved my life.

Lastly, to Eden for reminding me on a daily basis how to love unconditionally and to Jill, for being the string to my balloon.

Table of Contents

Foreword

I have had the pleasure of knowing Randy for over twenty years. We met at a conference where speakers from around the country had gathered to showcase their message before colleges. Randy's sincerity and caring heart, as well as his passion and desire to make a difference, resonated with me from our first interaction onward. Over the years, we have formed a close friendship.

Many years ago, Randy shared with me a moving story. He spoke about ego as it relates to a sea turtle literally taking him for a ride! Randy's tale captured me—I was completely captivated. Sometimes in your life, when people tell a story, you immediately realize it's one you'll always remember. With this book, Randy brings this story and its message to life. Through the teachings in this book, we begin to see how when we let ego get in our way, when our ego has us grasping to try and control people, things or outcomes, *there's simply nothing better than learning to let go*... because grasping is the very thing that keeps us trapped.

It's a gift this book is being put forward into the world. Who better than Randy to share these teachings? His humility, honesty, thoughtfulness and joyful presence comes through in his words, insights and storytelling.

Most people don't walk around self-identifying as in need of improving their self-esteem. Yet it is *most people* who would benefit from the message in this book.

Ego is elusive. We battle to let go of it, and as soon as we do, it's easy to get lost in ego by surprise again. I'll share with you a concept about ego that was eye-opening for me. I have another friend who was telling me about his experience "catching his ego." On a long drive, he chose to be aware of his thoughts and realized he was concerned about what other people were thinking of him. He realized, "Oh, there's my ego, being concerned about how others will perceive me. I've spotted you, ego, I found you out, I've got you cornered!" Yet when he said to himself, "I've got you, ego! I've got you cornered," what he didn't realize is his ego had *him*. In other words, *I've* got you ego…that's all ego.

This is exactly why I say ego is elusive. By its very nature, ego is a blind spot. It's so difficult to let go and detach from it. To cleanse ourselves of it. Yet doing so is the *very thing* that's most liberating and perspective-giving for us.

If you want to look in the mirror and truly love the person reflecting back at you, then turn this book into a workbook. Take action, and bring these teachings to life—in your own life. You're the only one who will ever be in the driver's seat of your own life. It's time to start steering…in a direction *you* want to go. This book is a helpful roadmap if you're lost or just wanting a better path to happiness.

When I was younger, I did not have strong self-esteem. I was quiet; I was shy. Fortunately, I learned from a top-level master Jiu-jitsu instructor an exercise to help me believe in myself and release the limiting low self-esteem thoughts I was having. He asked me to simply look in the mirror and say my name, followed by "You are a great person" one time each night right before bed. Then, when your head hits the pillow, he said to say, "And so It Is."

The master explained that at first, I may not believe what I was saying to myself in the mirror. He said that if stayed consistent, however, I would find my beliefs about myself change as my subconscious mind began to shift. It worked for me. I grew to see myself as a great person, and the more my self-esteem grew, the more I was able to detach from my ego. I was able to just *live*, happy and confident from the inside out. My life transformed.

My transformation was all internal. That's what this book is all about. I came to a place where I looked in the mirror and felt a smile and joy. *That* is transformation. It doesn't mean I got a new job or a new girlfriend immediately. It means I felt better about who I was. Externally, there was a ripple effect of change. When we change internally, it's reflected in changes externally. My friends and the people around me started to change for the better, almost magically without effort. The transformation also manifested in my confidence to take risks and go after the things I wanted in life. But the greatest gift was really internal—the person I get to live with every day is someone I actually love.

Finding freedom from within is the only way to true freedom. And it begins with cultivating a healthy self-esteem, which allows for more ease and shedding the entrapment of ego. The open state of being, stemming from true self-esteem, allows for greater perspective, greater insight, greater wisdom…and essentially, a greater sense of freedom and happiness.

That's what this book is here to help us do.

~Gary Tuerack, Founder and Chief Visionary,
The National Society of Leadership and Success

The Ego Cleanse

Introduction

"Yesterday I was clever, so I wanted to change the world. Today I am wise, so I am changing myself." ~Rumi

Our society has sold us a lie. We have been taught from an early age that if you have the "right" car, the "right" label on your shirt, the "right" job, the "right" number on the scale, then you have esteem. We have been taught that ego and self-esteem are the same thing, connected to each other. That all those outside *things* make us who we are. And it's just not true.

When I developed my self-esteem workshop, I searched for a memorable way to help people define self-esteem and build it for themselves by making some simple changes in their lives. This book is the result. It's a tried-and-true compilation of things I have learned over the course of 30+ years enhancing my own self-esteem and as a therapist and university administrator, helping others do the same. Before we get any further along, however, I want to be clear on the difference between *simple* and *easy*. While putting the ideas in this book into practice is simple, it is definitely *not* easy!

My journey toward enjoying a higher sense of self-esteem has been a long one. Very long. In fact, I'm hoping you don't have as far to go as I did. I come from a place where I had no self-esteem whatsoever. On May 16th, 1984, my self-esteem was so low that I was sitting in the bathroom with a knife in my hand, debating which wrist to slice open first.

I was ready to die. But instead, something inside made me reach out for help. I called a hotline because I thought I had no one else to turn to. Weeks later, I found an amazing therapist who helped me start my new journey. I met people through support groups who understood what I was going through. I started realizing I had feelings and that they were okay.

During this long journey back from the brink, I learned that I wasn't, in fact, a "stupid" person or a "worthless" person and I began to build my self-esteem and realize it had nothing to do with my outside world. It's taken me a long time to get to the point where I am now, and it's time to share all that I've learned. Today, as a professional speaker, I travel around the United States talking to people about how to make better choices and build their self-esteem.

I consider myself to be a success story and I know that if *I* can go from where I was to where I am, you can go anywhere you want. There are no limits to what you can accomplish if you just get out of your own way and start treating yourself with dignity and respect. If you're feeling stuck, stagnant, or complacent, you'll find some tools here to help shake things up for the better. If you feel the desire for more—more connection, more peace, a greater sense of wellbeing—but don't know how to get there, this book is for you.

Life can seem like a maze sometimes. There are all these paths jutting off in a million different directions, and we could all use some kind of guide. Without one, it's often easier to not choose any path at all—to play small and remain on the sidelines.

If you are feeling compelled to do more and be more, with greater self-awareness and increased self-confidence, you'll benefit from this short guidebook. I wrote it for anyone who wants to feel better about who they are and where they fit in the world. For anyone who wants a better sense of self—to wake up in the morning and feel you genuinely admire the person in the mirror. Really, I wrote it for everyone.

Imagine the process of raising self-esteem and self-growth like this: you're in a valley looking up at a mountain. There are a lot of people around you in the valley who say, "Wow, that's a beautiful sight." Eventually, you find it's not enough to just enjoy the sight of the mountain. You get a calling, a whisper inside yourself. It says, "I need to climb that mountain."

The other people in the valley warn you: "No, you don't want to do that. You could hurt yourself. Just stay down here with us, we'll be fine." But your inner voice won't stop. It keeps saying, "I have to climb."

So, you climb, and it's difficult and at times you feel like you're going to fall, but finally, you get to a plateau high above the valley. You look out at the view and say, "Wow, this view is *amazing*." Then, you meet other people who are on that same plateau. You're talking to each other, you feel connected, and you have the same perspective. It's a great feeling. You've achieved something special!

After some time, the same voice reappears inside of you. It's very clear when it announces, "I need to climb more." You hear a familiar message from the people on your plateau: "No, no, we are fine here. Climbing higher is really hard and you could hurt yourself." Never mind them, you need to climb.

You grapple and struggle to the next plateau, and it's even more difficult along the way. It's steeper, and it's harder to get there, and it takes more energy. But once you arrive at the next level, you are amazed, even astonished: "Wow, now *that's* a view." You feel so proud of yourself for your accomplishment and meet a few new people that you have an even stronger connection with. There aren't as many as there were on the lower plateau, but there are still some people up there, and they are all quite remarkable in their own unique ways.

Still, some of us are called to go even higher to that next level. Each time we climb, it's steeper, more dangerous, more challenging, and there are fewer people to greet us once we arrive. But the view is all the more breathtaking each time.

When you ask, "Is the journey worth it?" the answer is that we could probably be happy enough just staying on our plateau. But the deeper truth is you want to get to that next level in your life, and there's no turning off your inner voice. Yes, it is difficult. Yes, it is going to hurt. There's always the potential for falling. Climb anyway.

It's time to start treating yourself like your own best friend so you can experience the next magnificent view in your life.

Climb with me.

To you, the reader:

I am honored and humbled that you have chosen to read my book. It has been in the works for a very long time. As you go through the pages you will see that the book is imperfect. I wanted it to be real and even raw...as if you and I were having an actual in-person conversation. This book is about *celebrating* our imperfection. It is about looking past what's "wrong" with us and instead, shining a light on what's right and moving forward to make ourselves better.

My hope is this book will help put things into perspective for you and help you build a more solid sense of self-esteem by defining it in a different way and giving you the tools you need to make that happen. I wish you all the best that life has to offer, and I hope to meet you at some point down the road.

Section One: The Continuum

Today, many people in our society tend to confuse self-esteem with ego. The two are put together as one concept, linked and even interchangeable in many people's minds. I believe this is wrong. Ego and self-esteem are not connected. They have completely different definitions. In fact, I believe they are on opposite ends of a continuum.

Picture this idea in your mind. Place ego on one side of a line and self-esteem on the other. Because it's a continuum, all of us are somewhere on that line; very few people are totally ego, and very few have total self-esteem. As a continuum, how you are feeling at any given moment can shift to one side or the other. One day, you feel like you're moving more toward the self-esteem end. Other days, you feel less confident, act in more of an egotistical way and start moving the other direction. Your sense of self-esteem is not static and once you become more aware of this concept, you will have a better idea of where you are on the continuum. I do believe that, as you start this journey, it is not as important *where* you are on the continuum as it is which *direction* you're pointing in.

Chapter 1: Ego and Self-Esteem

"The greatest thing in the world is to know how to belong to oneself." ~Michel de Montaigne, Complete Essays

Ego: Your Outside World

One time, a commercial came on television that caught my attention. The message was, "Grow more hair and gain self-esteem!" I thought, "WHAT?! My self-esteem depends on how many follicles I have??" I'm sorry to say, but your self-esteem has nothing to do with how much hair you have on your head. Self-esteem has nothing to do with that number on the scale. Self-esteem has to do with how *you* feel about *you*, regardless of how you look, what you have, or how many "followers" you have on your social media platforms.

Before we talk about where you are on the continuum, let's take a closer look at the ego side of it. When I define ego, I am talking about defining yourself by everything that's going on in your *outside* world: what kind of car you drive, how much money you make, what kind of job you have, the label on your clothes— those are things that are ego-based. This is a completely different definition of ego from the Freudian definition. I'm talking about ego more in the way of the Buddhists, who see it as the illusion of the self.

Whenever you open up a magazine or look at your TV, what you see are ego images, products and activities that are supposed to make you feel better about yourself. But really, when you look at it honestly, do these things *really* make you feel better about who you are? No. They may give you a short-term burst of "Wow, I'm really something," but does the car you drive actually enhance who you are as a person?

Buying a nice car to impress others is just your ego taking charge. Sure, some people work hard and buy a nice car to reward themselves as a gift for their hard work. And that's great! But sometimes there's a fine line between rewarding yourself for a job well done and just showing off.

Self-Esteem: What's Going on Inside

Let's take a look at self-esteem. Self-esteem is what's going on inside, how you feel when you look at yourself in the mirror. There's no other way to measure it. No one else can tell you how much self-esteem you have.

There's no scale you can step on that will tell you your self-esteem level, so let's repeat this key idea: the only true measure of your self-esteem is how you feel about that person looking back at you when you make eye contact with the mirror. *That* is your level of self-esteem.

There are a lot of individuals in the news or on television who are examples of blatant, pure ego. There are some people where it is just apparent, like some reality TV stars, or the iconic *Mad Men* character Don Draper. But when I think of a person on the other side of the continuum, someone who represents pure self-esteem, Mother Teresa comes to mind. She was a person who had very few personal possessions and who wanted to be of service, to help people. Gandhi. Jesus. There are dozens of people from our history who epitomized these ideals, but because someone with high self-esteem doesn't need outside recognition to enjoy a sense of wellbeing, there are probably so many more out there that we just never hear about at all. Teachers, for example, or first responders.

One of the things I see from many people I've met, however, is a lack of confidence. "Could I be more? Could I do more?" without that solid sense of "I'm okay with who I am and what I'm doing right now." There are a lot of folks doing great work in the world who nevertheless doubt themselves because they're unable, for example, to buy a nicer car or more expensive labels. The whole "keeping up with the Joneses" mentality is eating away at our society.

That's who this book is for—the ones who really want a sense of inner peace but are not sure how to achieve it. I'm hoping they read this and say, "Yes!" and see my message about the value of self-esteem as a total affirmation of who they are and why they became a teacher or a firefighter or a nurse. I'd like people to say to themselves, "Buying into all that hype out there isn't necessary. It doesn't matter that I can't afford that label; I'll go to a discount store and get something that's comfortable, because what I wear doesn't define me. I'm defined by what my motives are, by what my values are. Not by the stuff I purchase, or by the number on the scale."

Self-esteem is all about finding your value internally rather than externally.

"What I'm looking for is not out there, it is in me."
~Helen Keller

Binaries

There are some clear differences between ego and self-esteem. The ego is all about defining yourself by your zip code, your shoes—the status things that Madison Avenue wants us to think will build our self-esteem, yet never really do the job.

Think about confidence versus cockiness, for example. Cockiness is based on ego. Confidence comes from solid self-esteem. They can sometimes look the same in theory, but the two qualities are so very different when you encounter them in real world situations.

There are a lot of binaries like this one when you look at the ego/self-esteem continuum. Humble versus humiliated is another one. The difference is how much ego is involved. "Oh my, what are people going to think of me?" is the humiliated ego talking after something has gone wrong. Humble is, "Wow, I am going to learn a lot from this experience, because I really messed up."

Self-esteem is solid, whereas ego is fragile. You can give someone an ego boost, or take away someone's ego, but you cannot give someone self-esteem or take it away. That's the beautiful part. It is earned and valued by ourselves, not by anyone else.

The whole purpose of this discussion is to make people aware of where they are on the continuum and help them to make little changes to move toward the self-esteem side. When people go on diets and say, "I'm going to lose ten pounds in a month," I think to myself, "Hmm, what's your motive? Is it about health or just dropping weight? Would it be better to just alter your eating habits a little bit? How about just switching from white to brown rice?" Or, "Rather than having a sandwich, have a salad."

It's easier to make little healthy changes than massive adjustments. Building self-esteem is the same way. Make little incremental changes instead of huge leaps.

"When you do not seek or need external approval, you are at your most powerful." ~Caroline Myss

Ego in Pop Culture

Consider the various reality TV stars out there who just keep appearing on one show after another. What do they *do*? What is their value besides their high-status life or their so-called fame? They seek fame as a way to define themselves and at times it's really painful to watch. Now, I don't know any of them, so I'm not making judgments on who they are. I'm looking at the lifestyle they portray as being successful and happy. The question is, are they really happy? People try to gain self-esteem from money, yet seventy percent of lottery winners say they wish they had never bought their winning ticket. They thought money was going to be their solution, but it doesn't have that power. Money often ends up harming people more than helping them. If you think of money only in terms of what it can buy or how you can use it to impress others, that's a house of cards. But if you think of it in terms of, "Wow, I can do some really great things with this but it's not who I am," you'll most likely be okay.

The ones who don't regret buying the winning lottery ticket are the ones who may or may not still live in the same house after they win. They might have a nicer car, but it doesn't change them as people. When it comes to money and self-esteem, it matters how you view it, and how you use it. Money is not going to *fix* you. It's not going to make you "something," but it can definitely be an enhancement.

> *"You are who you are when nobody's watching."*
> *~Stephen Fry*

There's No "It"

People are always looking for "it," whether it's the relationship, the house, the job, the salary, the car, the shoes. They're looking for *that one thing* that will make them okay, once and for all. The problem is, *there's no it*. It doesn't exist. The "it" is inside.

I was on a plane one time, and because I travel so much, I got upgraded to first class. I was sitting next to a man who was dressed impeccably. His shoes were probably worth more than everything I had on. We started talking. He asked, "So, what do you do?" I said, "I teach people about self-esteem." I told him the difference between ego and self-esteem and took him through some of the things I've learned. He said, "Wow, you know what? I just bought a second Mercedes, thinking that it was going to make me happy. It didn't. You are absolutely right. My car does not define who I am."

Lack of self-esteem is an overlooked reason for so much conflict in our world. People are out of touch with their inner worth and it makes them uneasy. They are trying to feel better, but often looking in the wrong place. They're searching or grabbing for things outside of themselves rather than inside, which can lead to behaving in ways that are selfish or harmful. For example, one underlying reason for misuse of alcohol and other drugs is low self-esteem. Thus, building self-esteem has significant lifelong benefits for the health and wellbeing of individuals, families, and society as a whole.

When I explain that I see ego and self-esteem as opposite sides of a continuum, my goal isn't to point out that some individuals have an ego "problem," or an ego "issue." By laying it out the way that I have, I want to give people a new perspective—to help them feel better about who they are and where they are in their lives.

"Do not pray for an easy life, pray for the strength to endure a difficult one." ~Bruce Lee

The Neutral People

There are some people on the continuum between ego and self-esteem who are just plain neutral. They're not high on self-esteem, yet they're not big ego people either. This might sound okay, but in reality, this middle ground isn't the best place to be, because the neutral folks don't feel very good about themselves or what's going on in their world. They often feel that life isn't great, and they have no control over it. They're hanging out in the middle, they don't have a sense of personal power or purpose.

To these folks, I say: *move*. Build something. It's okay. You'll find the tools and support you need once you start on the path. The alternative is to hang out in neutral forever. The good news for someone who is neutral is you won't have as much to overcome as you move along the continuum. Building your self-esteem is going to be easier than it might be for someone who has to wrestle with ego first.

Why do people slide into neutral? It's because we get very comfortable with the uncomfortable. We tend to just stay where we are, mostly out of fear. It's time to shake things up a bit. Make a small change to begin. Journal once a week. Read a book. Find a good therapist. Look for the little victories, not the huge conquests.

Chapter 2: Head to Heart

"A self is not something static, tied up in a pretty parcel and handed to the child, finished and complete. A self is always becoming." ~Madeleine L'Engle, A Circle of Quiet

Ego is the cacophony happening in your head. How many times have you had a decision to make and all these voices start talking in your head? Maybe you *should do that* and *what about this* and *how about that,* or the worst one, *"What are people going to think?"*

It gets very confusing.

Conversely, when you sit back and take a look at what's going on in your heart, *that's* where your self-esteem lies. How many times have you been in a situation where you had a decision to make, and you were battling back and forth in your head about what you should do, but in your heart and in your gut, you already knew the answer? Then, maybe about a week or a month later, you were able to look back at the situation and see that if you had gone with your gut

31

instinct in the first place, everything would have been okay?

There's an old Chinese proverb that says the longest and most difficult journey we ever make in our lifetime is from our head to our heart. It's a tough road to travel, and it's not going to happen overnight. Making the journey successfully is going to take practice and a long time to build up. It's kind of like running a marathon. A person doesn't wake up one morning and say, "Hmm, what do I want to do today? I think I'll go run a marathon!"

I know for me, if I woke up today and decided that I wanted to run a marathon, I'd probably collapse after three miles. It's not something I'd be able to do. Running a marathon takes time, patience and practice. It takes learning all the skills involved with running 26.2 miles. Building self-esteem is the same thing. It's not going to happen overnight.

The Effect of Building Your Self Esteem

No matter how long it takes, building self-esteem is one of the most worthwhile things you can ever do for yourself. Why? Because once your self-esteem is solid, your outlook on life brightens and becomes clearer. Take it from me—it's like living in a state of bliss. The pressure of life is taken off, because you've learned to allow yourself to be human. Now, that's not to say my life is perfect. It's not. Perfection is an illusion. I still have problems and issues that come up on a regular basis, but the way I deal with them is different because I've learned how to believe in myself. When you allow yourself to just be who you are without feeling like you have to be some other person to make those around you happy, life improves. It's about being happy with *yourself*. If the people around you aren't happy with who you are, change the people you're around.

Let's take a moment to talk about how challenging that can be in real life. It's no small thing to change the people you're around, but it may become necessary to your personal growth.

Back in the days when I was drinking and using drugs, I hung out with people who were drinking and using drugs. We were like-minded, we were doing the same things. Like attracts like. This is one of the hardest parts about raising self-esteem. When people do start to feel better about who they are, they start to realize that a lot of individuals they're around want to bring them back down.

They'll hear things from the old crowd such as: "Whoa, whoa, whoa, where are you going? You used to be such a good friend. What's wrong with you now?"

Nothing's wrong with you. You're evolving, you're changing. Some of your friends might have to change, too—you need to spend time with those who are going to accept the new you and support you in making changes. As I let go of the old friends, new ones started to take their place. They were new friends who did support my new lifestyle choices and helped me along the way.

> **"Great spirits have always encountered violent opposition from mediocre minds." ~Albert Einstein**

Change Is in the Air

I'm watching a lot of shows and movies right now that are reinforcing this idea of building real connections with others, friendships based not on ego or on surface similarities, but based on self-esteem. One good example of this is *A Million Little Things* on ABC. It's awesome. It's about these four guys who are best friends—they go to hockey games together, their families know each other, they get together often—and then one of them commits suicide. The others are deeply affected by the fact that they didn't know he was suffering. One of them says, "You know what? We only talk about weather, sports and news. We don't talk about what's really going on with us." I'm thinking, perfect! *This is exactly what I'm getting at.* All these examples are out there right now reinforcing this message. This lets me know I'm on the right track with this topic.

I want to have deep friendships with people, but it's hard to find guys who go beyond news, weather and sports in their conversations. Sure, I like talking about those things, but once in a while I want to talk about stuff like, "Hey, I'm feeling a little insecure today." Or, "Today I'm feeling really excited." A lot of men, and women, are uncomfortable with that kind of conversation. I want people to grasp these concepts so they're more genuine, and able to unleash what's already there. It's there, they're just keeping it in the gates. Let's open the gates!

Give yourself permission to ask for what you need from other people and trust that it'll be okay—you'll probably even receive the thing you asked for. That's one of the by-products of self-esteem: confidence and even peace.

"The better you feel about yourself, the less you feel the need to show off." ~Robert Hand

Mental Illness

For those with mental health issues, the number one thing to realize is that there's nothing *wrong* with you. You have a chemical imbalance in your brain, it's not like you did anything to cause that. I watch a lot of people with mental illness look at themselves and feel, "I'm defective, there's something wrong with me." *No.*

There are ways to move beyond this particular challenge. Today, we are in a society where it's accepted and discussed more than ever before. *It's okay to talk about* mental illness. It doesn't have to be a shadow thing. Find therapy and medication and things you can do to combat the mental health challenge you have, so you can get to a place to build your self-esteem.

Mental illness isn't an excuse to never work on yourself or avoid building a high-value life. I struggle with ADHD and an anxiety disorder, but I choose not to let it consume me or prevent me from reaching my goals. There are ways to overcome the obstacle of mental illness. It doesn't mean your life is over, and it does not have to define you. Get the help you need to become balanced.

Beware the "Quick Fix"

All these gimmicks are out there to show you a quick fix on how to build your self-esteem *now*. Be careful with these, because I don't think there *is* a quick fix. We live in a very quick fix society and it's time to put that attitude aside and to really take a look at the things that are important to us and help us grow as people.

Madison Avenue and the way advertising happens has a lot to do with people's overall lack of self-esteem, so we can't *buy* something to enhance it. These commercials tell us we're supposed to look a certain way. Consider the way they airbrush magazine images, for example. I love that some people are now saying, "Don't airbrush me! Let me be who I am." That's so empowering. I love to see this shift, because our society has been so into how we look, and what we do, and how much money we have that we've lost track of what's really important.

Also in the quick fix category are people using drugs or drinking excessively. I have yet to meet anyone who truly has high self-esteem who uses drugs. High self-esteem and drug use don't go well together. People only have to alter their state if they're not happy with the state they're naturally in.

Likewise, eating large amounts of sugar, compulsively overeating in general, smoking, compulsive gambling and other behaviors like these are so demeaning and self-defeating. It's really difficult to gain self-esteem while engaging in these behaviors.

Social Media

People will say, "Oh my gosh, I only got 20 likes!" Or, "I only have 53 followers!" With social media, it's all about the likes and the followers. That's your ego saying, "Look, I'm somebody because I have all these likes." No, it's a trap! That kind of external measurement does not define you.

For people who put their self-worth onto how many likes or how many followers they have, social media is so dangerous. It's another example of ego versus self-esteem. The number of friends I have on Facebook is not who I am, so I'd prefer to only stay "friends" with the people on that platform that I genuinely want to hear from.

To me, a friendship is not real until you pick up the phone and call someone, or meet them for coffee, a meal, or a day together. Social media is a trap that people can get caught up in—seeing their online life as their real life. It's not. It's a snapshot. It's a headline.

There's no meat to it; it's superficial. Getting lost in that world can be less than great, because that's not the real world. It's an ego world.

Chapter 3: The Hole

"We are a very creative species—we can use just about anything to anesthetize ourselves. But in doing so, we also remove ourselves from feeling the joy." ~Oriah Mountain Dreamer, The Invitation

I am very fortunate that I have an amazing family. Of course, we have our issues like any other family, but my dad's story is the ultimate American Dream story. He was raised in Minnesota and decided to be an accountant. He dropped out of college in his sophomore year to take care of his family. When my parents got married, my mom was 19, my dad was 21.

One winter, they went to California to visit my uncle. They left -10-degree weather and arrived in 72-degree weather. My mom said, "What are we doing in Minnesota? Let's move to California!" They packed up a three-year-old, a four-year-old, and $300 into a beat-up Chevrolet with no job waiting and drove. They found an apartment, and my dad got a job. He didn't like that job, so he got a better one. One of his accounting clients at the new firm was into real estate and property management and invited my dad to invest with him. He talked to my mom and she said, "Al, I heard real estate in L.A. is pretty good." This was in the mid-1960s. "Just do it." So, my dad invested and made some money. And invested again and made some more money.

My dad stopped working as an accountant and began managing properties. He did very well for himself by taking risks. It just clicked for him. I think both of my parents are proud of what they've done, and they're very philanthropic, which is great to watch. My dad made his fortune, and never did it at anyone else's expense. He's one of the good guys. He is proof to me that you can be a nice guy and still be successful.

My parents had those Midwestern values, but I was influenced by the L.A. 1980's atmosphere. I had my first car when I was 16 years old. I went to private schools and had everything a person is supposed to want. But I felt so empty; I didn't really know where I fit. My parents were always saying, "Do better in school, get better grades!" But I had a severe case of ADHD, and nobody ever diagnosed it. People would say, "Why can't you apply yourself? Randy, you're so smart, why can't you just get your homework done?"

My answer? *I don't know.* I really didn't know. I would sit there looking at a book, and my brain felt like it was shorting out. I wasn't able to do what I was supposed to be doing; I was really struggling. Today, we recognize ADHD and have solutions to address it, but back then we didn't really know what it was or how it was affecting people. I wasn't a star academically, I wasn't that good at sports. I liked playing, but I just wasn't that good.

So, I found my "thing" in alcohol and drugs. I didn't have to feel that pressure anymore; I didn't care. I started to build a persona in the party world, which is all ego. There is no self-esteem in the alcohol and drug world at all. It's more like, "If I have more cocaine than you, then I'm better than you. If I have more girlfriends, I am really somebody." It was and is so hollow.

I felt like there was this huge hole inside of me, and the only way I thought I could fill it up was with more stuff, and then with alcohol, and then with marijuana, and then with cocaine.

I realize now that we all have a hole, not just addicts. Everybody. The more we try to fill it up, the bigger it gets. And any time we attempt to fill it up with cars, clothes, alcohol, women, men, jewelry, or "likes and followers," it just gets bigger.

So, what do we do about it? Accept it. Let it be there. If we let the hole be what it is, if we let ourselves *have* our hole, understand that it's a part of us, and respect it for being there because having it is just part of our experience as humans, we can find peace. Some of the greatest musicians in the history of the world have depression or anxiety issues, yet they're using their hole as a way to find their art. Again, *we all have that hole*. We've all been damaged in one way or another growing up. So, the best thing to do is just accept it. We're all imperfect beings, and when we just let that hole be, it doesn't get bigger. Respect the hole. Breathe into it. Let it be what it is. I have also found that when we build our self-esteem, the hole actually gets smaller. It will never be completely gone, but it can get smaller when we truly take care of ourselves.

The Choices We Make

I was in a band when I was 19 years old. We were really good and were even asked to headline a festival in Portland. I remember looking out at that sea of three or four thousand people, and thinking, "Wow, I could see doing this the rest of my life, being on stage performing for people."

We recorded a demo tape in a studio and sent it out to all the record companies in the country. We got a call back from Albatross Records in Seattle saying, "We need an opening band for Heart on their West Coast tour. If the fans like you on the West Coast, we're going to put you on the national tour." Wow! What an opportunity! The guys in the band said to me, "If we're going to do this, you have to quit the drugs. So, do you want to quit the band, or quit the drugs?" And I said, "Screw you, I'll go find another band."

So, that was that.

I use this story to illustrate that we are a product of the choices we make. When you break it down to the core, that's all we really are. Every choice we make leads us to where we are right now.

The end of this particular story isn't a sad one, however. Even though I did choose drugs over my band, I found out, way back when I was 19 years old, that I wanted to be on stage, touching the lives of hundreds, thousands, or hundreds of thousands of people. And that's exactly what I get to do now as a speaker.

Which Direction Are You Pointed In?

Let's go back to our continuum. On this continuum, we have ego on one side and self-esteem on the other. It's important to make an honest assessment of where you are right now. Are you more toward the ego side, more toward the self-esteem side, or are you somewhere in the middle? It doesn't matter where you are on that continuum; what really matters is which direction you're pointed in. Are you doing the things necessary to build your self-esteem today, or are you doing the things today that are simply reinforcing your ego?

Only *you* are going to know which direction you're going in. Again, no one can tell you. *You* are the only one who can make this distinction. The starting point of any journey is realizing where you are when you start. There's no right or wrong place to be when you begin. The most important part is pointing in the right direction and taking the first step.

Section Two: Obstacles

Now that we have the continuum concept down, I want to move on, helping you learn how to build your self-esteem. There are some simple ways you can do this. But before we get into these ideas, we need to address the ways we tear ourselves down. We need to take a look at our destructive inner voices before we can truly build ourselves up. So, let's examine some obstacles we face.

Turning Hurdles into Walls

Obstacles are a part of life. They are our hurdles. Some are small hurdles, others are larger, but often we turn those hurdles into walls, and the walls are much more difficult to get over. We need to let our hurdles be hurdles. Life is a lot easier when we make this switch, because we can always find support around us to get over the hurdles.

For example, I had this thought in my mind: "I'm too ADHD, I can't write this book!" Huge wall. But a better way to frame the same idea is, "Yes, I will have a really difficult time writing a book, but if I can find a ghostwriter to help me put the presentation into book form, I can do this!" That new thought turned the wall into a hurdle that I can now overcome.

We turn hurdles into walls by using very simple words and phrases that end up ripping ourselves to shreds. Once you hear what these obstacle words and phrases are, you'll see how often you tend to use them.

Years ago, when I was still pretty big on the ego side, I would wake up in the morning and look at myself in the mirror and say, "Boy, are you ugly! Look at you, you're so fat and no wonder you don't have a girlfriend..." and blah, blah, blah. My head was just taking off in all these different condescending directions and awful ideas. No wonder I didn't feel good about myself.

Back then, I poured poison into myself when I hadn't even been up for 15 minutes!

If anybody talked to me the way I talked to myself on a regular basis, we would *never* have been friends. I would not have allowed someone as cruel as I'd been to myself in the same room with me! Yet for 35 years, this voice in my head followed me around all day, every day, calling me a fat, lazy, stupid, ugly loser who never did anything right. That awful little voice said I was never good enough and kept telling me I *should have done this* and *should have done that.* Finally, I had enough. Our self-talk is so important and a vital step in building self-esteem.

Your Own Best Friend

Back when I was in college, there were times when I would study hard for a test and get a C. I would say things to myself like, "You are so stupid! I can't believe you got a C on that test. You should drop out of school. You're too lame to pass this class anyway." Now, if my best friend studied hard for a test and got a C, my response would be completely different. I would say something like, "That's okay. You did your best. Getting a C doesn't make you a stupid person. You'll do better next time."

That's why it's time to start treating ourselves like our best friend rather than our worst enemy. I mean, when you actually think about it honestly, would you let anyone talk to you the way you talk to yourself sometimes? Probably not.

Chapter 4: Can't

"Argue for your limitations and, sure enough, they're yours." ~Richard Bach, Illusions: The Adventures of a Reluctant Messiah

There are simple words and phrases we use all the time that are obstacles to building self-esteem, and it's time to get rid of them. The first one I want to discuss is *can't*. Can't is a word that immediately turns a hurdle into a wall. How many times have you said to yourself, "I can't lose weight, I can't change my eating patterns, I can't get a better job, I can't get out of this relationship, I can't quit drinking, I can't stop smoking?" Can't is a word that creates a huge obstacle that is almost impossible to get over. And we keep reinforcing and reinforcing the idea that something is impossible until finally, we start believing it.

Do you think Michael Jordan ever went up to the free throw line and said, "I can't make this shot?" Of course not. Every time he went up to that free throw line, he said, "I'm going to make this." And the majority of the time, he made the shot.

It's time for us to do this for ourselves. Rather than continue to knock ourselves down, it's time we start building ourselves up. *Can't* is a word that needs to be taken out of your vocabulary. The first step is to become aware of how often you say it, then replace it. Use another word, maybe a phrase that's more honest. How about *it's difficult?* "It's difficult to lose weight, it's difficult to quit smoking. But yes, I can do it!"

Take a thoughtful look at what's really going on when you use the word *can't*. Many times, the honest answer is, "I'm afraid to" or sometimes, "I don't want to." Instead of "I *can't* lose weight," begin getting extremely honest and say, "I don't *want* to exercise and eat better right now. Maybe in a month I'll change my mind, but for now I don't want to."

Open up your awareness to your thoughts and start looking at words and phrases that might not be serving you very well. You can look at behaviors later on. Think of this section of the book as the seeds to this concept, an invitation to eventually look beyond these words and phrases to habits and actions that might be holding you back from building your self-esteem.

The obstacle words you're using are not going to be the same one's other people use. The key is finding your own individual path; that's the coolest part. Look for what works or doesn't work for you. Then look for what you *can* do, rather than what you feel you're not able to do. Obstacles go beyond words and phrases, but it's up to you to figure out what your patterns and behaviors are throughout your day.

Chapter 5: Are You Shoulding All Over Yourself?

"...My wish for you is that you feel no need to constrict yourself to make other people comfortable."
~Ta-Nehisi Coates, Between the World and Me

"I *should* quit smoking, I *should* eat better, I should lose weight, I should work harder, I should play harder, I should do this, I should do that. I should, should, should..."

All we end up doing is shoulding all over ourselves.

It's time to give ourselves a break. Let's take a look at what *should* does. Using this word, especially when you use it a lot, is like taking a mental sledgehammer and knocking yourself over the head, saying, "I'm not good enough."

"I should be getting B's, I should be getting A's." What that says is, "I'm not good enough. What I'm doing isn't good enough."

"I should lose weight" says: "Where I'm at today is not good enough. I need to do more."

I grew up with a lot of *it's not good enough.* Fortunately, I learned it was time to give myself a break. The good news is when I let myself be who I am and let myself be right where I'm at, I can start moving forward. If I'm constantly pulling myself to this place where I think I *should* be, I'm not going to make much progress.

Should is one of those words that needs to go. My ADHD made it very difficult to complete my schoolwork and do well on tests, so I beat myself up over things that I really had no control over. Today, I rarely use *can't* or *should.* I'm sure I slip up now and then, but these words are just not a part of my vocabulary anymore. I rarely look at situations and life with these words; I've had over 30 years of practice making this change. That's the thing—it takes time. You're not going to get it down right at the beginning. Be patient and loving with yourself as you're going through this process of drawing attention to your obstacle words. Again, be patient with yourself like you would be patient with your best friend.

Chapter 6: There Is No Try

"Fall down seven times, stand up eight."
~Japanese proverb

Try is one of those devastating words that keeps us from making a full commitment to an action. How many times have you said, "I'll try to quit drinking, I'll try to lose some weight, I'll try to go back to school, I'll try to be on time, I'll try to do better?"

Trying doesn't work. Trying is lying. During my presentations, I'll ask for a volunteer. I ask them to raise their arm. And they raise their arm. Then I ask them to *try* to raise their arm. They invariably raise their arm. I say, "No, don't raise your arm, just *try* to raise your arm." They look at me with a confused expression on their face and usually don't raise their arm or move it just a little bit. Then I say, "See? You either raise your arm or don't raise your arm. There's no such thing as *trying* to raise your arm."

In the immortal words of Yoda, *"Do. Or do not. There is no try."* And I totally agree with that. "Trying" is a cop out. Trying is a way to not take responsibility for doing your best and, as a result, it (whatever *it* is) not working out. Sometimes in life we do the best we can, and things still don't work out. The team that didn't win the Super Bowl didn't "try" to win. They did their very best and didn't score as many points as their opponent. But still, for the rest of their lives, they can say they played in the Super Bowl.

Failure

Our society says that failure is a horrible thing, and says something profound about us as individuals. Well, I don't know about you, but I've learned the *most* out of some of my failures. Failing is the way that I learn how to be a better person. Sometimes I need to fail in order to truly succeed, so we need to give ourselves a break with the concept of failure.

Last year, I went back to work at a university in California. I worked with someone I had known for years and thought it would be fun working with this person. Shortly after I got there, however, I realized he was not who he portrayed himself as being. For him, and he stated this, "Perception is the most important thing to focus on." I knew at that moment this might not work out. Over and over again in the next few months, he would stop me from doing my job and ask me to behave in ways that were outside my integrity and comfort zone. I persisted because the students and other staff members I worked with told me how great I was doing and how much of a difference I was making on campus. I was doing things that no one had done before in my position.

Then one day, five and a half months into my six-month probationary period, my boss called me into his office for an "update" meeting and fired me. No warning, no mention that I was doing anything wrong before that. He just told me I wasn't a good fit for the department and he fired me.

I was really upset. I was upset for my family who counted on my paycheck. I was sad for the students who I wasn't going to be able to help anymore. At first, I was *really* angry at my boss for being so smallminded and dysfunctional.

Here's the truth, though: If I was still in that position, I would not have written this book. I would not have moved from California to the place I've always wanted to live. In the moment, of course, it can be tough to see the big picture. Even though it seemed I was a "failure" at my job at the time, I know that I wasn't a failure. I did a great job and I helped a lot of people, but I wasn't a good fit for that particular role. My former boss needed someone he could control and someone who would do the bare minimum to make his superiors happy with his "numbers." As one of my coworkers told me, "You went too far beyond your job description." That experience led me to where I am today. I have dozens of stories like this. I could talk about my addiction, my college career, other positions I've held where I could look at one viewpoint and see myself as a failure, but I'm not. Each one of those experiences made me stronger and helped shape me into the person I am today.

Chapter 7: If Only and What If?

"Your playing small does not serve the world."
~Marianne Williamson

Another obstacle phrase I see people use quite often is *if only:* "If only I had more money I'd be happy, if only I lost weight I'd be attractive, if only I had a relationship I'd be complete." *If only* is another trap we fall into to avoid giving ourselves credit for where we are in the present moment.

If only is one of those things that society tells us: "If only I had a nicer car, if only I had better clothes, then I'd be okay." This is the cart before the horse type of trick. It tells us, "When I get *there,* then I'll be okay. When I get *there,* I'll be alright." It's just a way for you to not be content where you are.

I heard a saying one time that resonated with me: *When our there becomes a here we simply obtain another there, which again seems better than here.* I know it's a little confusing. You might have to rewind or reread a couple of times to get it, but basically what it says is if we are always looking for something

61

outside of ourselves to be happy, we're never truly going to be satisfied with what we have.

I grew up in nice neighborhoods in Southern California around a lot of people who had a lot of *stuff*. It was amazing to me that no matter how much stuff they had, it always seemed they needed more in order to be truly happy. I watched these people struggle and struggle and struggle, and they never became happy. Why? Because they kept looking *outside of themselves* for things to be okay.

We need to go within to truly find our happiness. This has nothing to do with our outside world. I've learned that true happiness is from the inside out, not the outside in. Sure, material things can be nice, but it doesn't make us who we are. Keep in mind that statistic I mentioned earlier: 70% of lottery winners say they regret buying the ticket.

The "What Ifs"

I know a lot of people who use the "what ifs." They fill their lives with them. "What if I ask her out and she says no?" "What if I study really hard and I fail this class?" As a result, they start making their decisions based on fear. When you make your decisions based on fear, it's really hard to move forward. Fear paralyzes and "what if" is a sure-fire way to stoke the flames of fear.

Fear can also be a motivator, but what I find for people who are stuck in the what ifs, it tends to be a paralyzer more than a motivator. So, it's important to see how often you use the *what ifs* and start getting them out of your vocabulary.

Getting stuck in the what ifs is not a way for us to build our self-esteem. It's a way we keep ourselves down. It keeps us from even *attempting* to go over a hurdle, and now all of the sudden it's a wall, and we end up slamming into it.

Unfortunately, some of us have been reinforcing these words and these phrases in our minds, and out loud, for years, even decades. Changing these thought patterns is not going to happen overnight. The what ifs and other obstacle phrases we discussed here are not going to just shut themselves off.

The Yeah-Buts

"Yeah, but..." is a way of not taking personal responsibility for what's going on in your life. "You were ten minutes late." "Yeah, but traffic was really bad today." Here's a better way to address this same situation: Leave a little earlier, or say, "I'm really sorry I'm late. Traffic was worse than I anticipated." That's different than the "yeah, but..." which is a way to deflect responsibility.

Self-esteem is about owning who you are and the choices you make each day. This doesn't mean you have to be perfect; far from it. Perfection is an illusion. Expecting 100% of yourself all the time is such a depleting way to live. It's exhausting and actually unrealistic.

Chapter 8: The *Have-To's*

"I prefer to be true to myself, even at the hazard of incurring the ridicule of others, rather than to be false, and to incur my own abhorrence." ~Frederick Douglass

Many people tell themselves, "I have to go to work," "I have to get up at 7:00," or "I have to go to practice." Yet the truth is: No, you don't. You *get to* go to work, you *get to* wake up early to get your day started, you *get to* go to practice. No matter how bleak you see your circumstances as being, it could always be worse. Look at the opportunities in your life as blessings instead of chores. As I sit here writing this book, I could easily say, "I have to write this book." But the truth is I *get to* write this book. I get to spend time writing today. What a blessing!

The point is, it is amazing to me how tightly some people hold on to the notion of "I have to," and not open themselves to another perspective. The lesson is that as you are moving through this process of rethinking some things and considering new ideas, you are probably going to find walls that will be really difficult to get through. My suggestion is to simply let

65

the hardest ones go for now. Leave the "have to" alone, if it's just too overwhelming for you. Look at the "shoulds" instead, or the "can'ts."

Focus on what works for you, at this point in your life.

Start Noticing Your Obstacle Words

Are you more of a "should-er?" Or more of a "can't" person? Is "try" big for you? How about those "have to's?"

As we lay all of these out, the question is which ones are more prominent in your life? Becoming more aware of what they are will be helpful. *Then* you can start making some changes and asking people to support you in that shift.

Find a friend or someone you trust to help you out and start to become more conscious of how often you use these obstacle words and phrases in your life. Slowly get rid of them and let your friends assist you. Let your friends know, "Hey, I want to get rid of the tries and the can'ts and the shoulds, so when you hear me saying these things, would you let me know?" It's amazing how much support you are going to get when you start turning these things around in your life.

Up to this point in the book, we've been looking at ways that we tear ourselves down. Now, it's time to get into the good stuff. Let's start looking at ways that we can build ourselves up.

Section 3: Building Self-Esteem

To build self-esteem, there are specific tools you can use. In the pages that follow, I lay out a blueprint of how you can begin to build your self-esteem. I do this by separating the "self" into four different parts, physical, mental, emotional, and spiritual. I believe that if we nourish and exercise the four parts of self on a regular basis and in a healthy way, we're going to feel better about who we are, and our self-esteem will naturally strengthen.

Chapter 9: Physical Self

"What the caterpillar calls the end of the world, the master calls a butterfly." ~Richard Bach, Illusions: The Adventures of a Reluctant Messiah

We will address how to nourish and exercise the physical self first, because I think it's the easiest one to illustrate. How do we nourish our physical self? With food. That's an easy one. *How* we nourish ourselves with food makes a big difference in our energy level during the day. If I wake up in the morning and I'm 15 minutes late and I throw down three cups of coffee and a couple of Twinkies, is that nourishing? No. Not in a healthy way.

Then, I get to work and lunchtime arrives. There's no time for lunch and I've got too much to do, so I'm just going to have a Mountain Dew and some of those cracker and peanut butter sandwich things, and that's going to be my lunch. Halfway through the afternoon I'll have a Snickers bar and an energy drink because I'm starting to get a little tired. Then when I get home from work, I don't have a lot of energy, so I'm just going to pop something in the microwave and swallow it without really tasting it.

How nourishing is that kind of routine for the physical self? How much energy are you truly going to have if *that's* the way you are nourishing yourself? Not a lot.

On the other hand, nourishing ourselves in a positive way does a lot for our esteem and our overall health. I'm not a big fan of "diets," but I am a fan of altering our food choices. When making changes, it is important to make small impactful changes rather than huge overnight changes. Again, treating ourselves like our own best friend.

We've heard our whole lives that breakfast is the most important meal of the day, and it is. In order to raise our self-esteem, it is important to have a balanced breakfast. No more, "I can't. I don't have time in the morning." Or "I know I should." Now is the time to see what you can do to make it happen. A balanced breakfast can be anything from a couple of eggs and toast to a protein shake with fruit to a couple of toaster waffles with peanut butter and a banana sliced on top. Oatmeal with peanut butter and banana or raisins. Experiment. Play around with what works for you. You'll find that once you get into a routine of waking up 10 minutes earlier, so you can make a healthy breakfast for yourself, you'll have more energy during the day and you'll feel better about yourself for doing something positive first thing in the morning.

"I do not exist to impress the world. I exist to live my life in a way that will make me happy." ~Richard Bach, Illusions: The Adventures of a Reluctant Messiah

Sleep

I find a lot of people I talk to are sleep deprived. They rarely get restful sleep, and there's a correlation between what we're feeding ourselves and how much sleep we're getting. I watch how much stress people are putting themselves under and it is amazing—not in a good way—what people are doing to themselves each week.

Make more time to sleep at night and give yourself the opportunity to nap when you need to. You're not a machine.

We really need to get our rest. I'm a big believer in naps; I think naps are so important. Sometimes my weekend revolves around taking an afternoon nap and that's important for me to rejuvenate myself and keep my energy level high.

Exercise

How do we exercise the physical self? There are lots of ways. There's running and swimming or walking or tennis, yoga, aerobics, weight lifting. For me to say, "Well, there's nothing I can do to exercise, there's nothing I like doing" is a cop out, because there's always something available to do. Have I really attempted everything out there? Probably not. So, it's important to find something that you enjoy doing that will exercise your physical self, no matter what it is. I attempted multiple types of exercise but didn't like any of them. It wasn't until I went to a fitness kickboxing gym that I found something I love and look forward to doing. So, keep at it. There's something out there you can do that is enjoyable for you.

If I decide that I'm going to run and you decide that you're going to swim, both are great options. It's not my place to say, "You're not really exercising because you are swimming. I'm a runner, that's the only way to exercise." Is it my place to do that? Absolutely not. It is not up to me to judge what's best for another person. All that matters is that you *are* exercising—you're actually doing it!

Again, building self-esteem does not happen overnight. This is something that takes time, it takes patience, and it takes practice. How we nourish and exercise our physical self is vital in feeling good about who we are. And it's the same with the other three parts of self.

Quick Tips and Ideas for Nourishing and Exercising Your Physical Self:

- Make small changes and make better eating choices instead of "going on a diet"
- Switch from white rice to brown rice
- Go from drinking soft drinks to water
- Take some time to figure out what foods best nourish your physical self, rather than eating things that fill a different kind of void
- Enjoy one glass of wine instead of two
- Drink more water
- Sleep is an important part of nourishing the physical self
- When it comes to exercise, there is no wrong way to do it; anything is better than nothing
- Go slow at the beginning
- Walk to the corner and back, swim, do yoga, tennis, box, bike, row or anything else that gets you moving

Chapter 10: Mental Self

"This above all: to thine own self be true."
~William Shakespeare, Hamlet

Nourishing and exercising the mental part of self is crucial, yet most people don't think about sleeping or doing a crossword puzzle as nourishing. This is a new way to think about exercising their mental self. As we introduce this idea, start to discover ways that you can give attention to this part of yourself.

Any time we open our minds to new ideas, any time we learn something new, we're exercising and nourishing the mental self. Sometimes the nourishment of the mental self is as simple as taking a nap or going for a walk to clear your head.

Follow Your Own Curiosity

There are a lot of tools available to nourish the mental self, it's just a matter of using the ones that interest you. Reading books that stretch you is a great idea, whether it's a fun book or just something you're intrigued by, like astronomy or medieval history. Follow your own curiosity. What do *you* want to read? What are you interested in?

Watching documentaries or movies can stimulate the mental part of self. Doing crossword puzzles or Sudoku is a phenomenal way to exercise this part of self—it's kind of like doing bicep curls for your brain.

There are a lot of healthy habits that have crossover when it comes to nourishing the mental self, such as taking that twenty-minute power nap. Making a habit of resting isn't just good for your mental self, it's also good for your physical and emotional self as well.

"Do you really want to look back on your life and see how wonderful it could have been had you not been afraid to live it?" ~Caroline Myss

Take a Class, Any Class

College students spend their time attending classes, writing papers, opening books and studying. If you are a college student, you're like a mental John Cena, buff mentally. You're exercising your mental self every day. For adults who are no longer in school, it can be a bit tougher, but if it would be helpful or fun for you, go take a class at a local college. Just one. Take a fun one to begin with. Take photography or creative writing, whatever looks interesting to you. You'll find it very stimulating for the mental self.

Quick Tips and Ideas for Nourishing Your Mental Self:

- Read books
- Take a class
- Take a nap
- Meditate
- Watch documentaries and shows that make you think
- Do Sudoku, crossword puzzles, word games, or strategy games

Chapter 11: Emotional Self

"There is a sacredness in tears. They are not the mark of weakness, but of power. They speak more eloquently than ten thousand tongues.

~Washington Irving

Turning our attention to our emotional selves is a tough one for a lot of people. We have a society that doesn't encourage feeling our feelings very well. In fact, I believe we live in a society that is emotionally anorexic. Most of the time when I say to people, "Hey, how are you feeling?" they reply, "I'm feeling good," or, "I'm feeling bad." Excuse me, but *good* and *bad* are not feelings. Even worse is when someone says, "I'm fine." *Fine,* to me, is shorthand for "F**ked up, Insecure, Neurotic and Egotistical! It's now time to start exploring and expressing our feelings.

Starting when we were little kids, we've been taught not to feel our feelings. Have you ever watched a little boy or a little girl about four or five years old get angry? I mean, they *really* get angry, and what do the parents do? They try to stuff that anger, they stifle it. Have you ever seen a little boy start crying? Their

81

entire being becomes sadness. And many boys are told to stop crying. We are told that showing emotion is a weakness, but I'm here to tell you that it is actually a strength. Some of the strongest, most confident people I know are able to feel and express their emotions.

Hurt Turned Sideways

From an early age, men are raised with the concept "Big boys don't cry." We stuff our feelings or, even worse, turn them sideways. If someone says something that hurts our feelings, instead of responding with, "Hey, what you said really hurt my feelings," we turn our hurt sideways so it comes out as anger and say, "Hey man, you really pissed me off. Say that again and I'll take you out." We have a tendency to turn our hurt and our sadness into anger.

Think about many of the world's problems today. World leaders and those in their countries often feel misunderstood, hurt, and frustrated, but instead of expressing those emotions, they express anger and take it out on those they believe have wronged them. If we talked about our feelings as they truly are, maybe we'd be able to have more positive dialogue and resolve our conflicts in a healthier way.

"People are afraid of themselves, of their own reality; their feelings most of all. You should stand up for your right to feel your pain." ~Jim Morrison

Who is Allowed to Express Anger?

Let's take a look at women and the messages they receive about feelings. From talking to women I know personally, and from working with dozens of women in therapy, what I find is women aren't allowed to have their anger. They're not allowed to be angry. They're told it doesn't look "ladylike"; it's not proper for a little girl to be angry. They're taught to stuff their anger.

As a result of these unhelpful messages, women turn their anger sideways and it tends to come out as sadness. If you're female and reading this, ask yourself: how many times have you been angry about something and ended up crying about it? Perhaps you didn't even know why you were expressing sadness. What was really going on is you were simply feeling angry.

Women tend to hold their anger inside, and it builds and it builds. They eat their anger, or they work their anger, or they overcompensate their anger. But eventually it will leak out. It's important to have your anger and to own it, because anger is a boundary, a way to say, "No. It is not okay for you to talk to me that way." Or, "It is not okay that you just did that." Women are taught, "You don't say anything." But anger is a human dignity, and it's important to own it and allow yourself to feel it, no matter which gender you happen to be.

Keep in mind there's a difference between anger and violence. Anger is an emotion. Violence is an action. I never advocate violent action, unless you're protecting yourself. But I always advocate for being okay with expressing your anger.

A lot of times, when we're getting in touch with our emotions, the pendulum can swing the other way and suddenly we feel way too strongly about someone bringing the wrong salad dressing or some other seemingly little thing. And it's okay. The pendulum will swing wildly for a bit. Be patient, it takes time for it to settle down.

We're emotional anorexics, and it's rarely possible to go directly into a healthy diet after struggling with an eating disorder. You have to ease your way into it. It's that way with all of these feelings.

Let's encourage more opportunities in our culture to talk about our feelings. As you're nourishing and exercising your emotional self, it helps to talk about your feelings. Find a good friend, a therapist, a member of the clergy, someone who is very comfortable talking about the full spectrum of feelings. Notice if you apologize for having feelings. If you start to cry in front of other people, do you say, "I'm sorry?" Why do we apologize for honestly showing an emotion?

I've seen it a half dozen times in the last week, where someone's been on a show, or something happens and they're crying for joy or for sadness, and they feel they have to apologize for it.

It goes back to how emotionally closed off our society is. When someone is genuinely showing emotion, they feel shame or embarrassment. They feel they need to apologize for it. Yet we don't smile and laugh and then say, "I'm sorry." So why do we do this on the other side of the emotion continuum, with fear, or sadness, or hurt? Crying is just as genuine as breaking out in laughter; showing your joy and showing your sadness are both valid. Consider what it would mean for you to celebrate both being able to laugh and to cry, and experience a genuine emotion without resistance or judgment.

Expression of the feeling is one thing; the other key is simply being able to identify what you're feeling. Can you say, "Wow, I'm feeling really sad right now?" It doesn't really matter if you cry or not. The question is are you able to identify, and fully feel, your emotions? Or do you stuff them down, deny them, eat through them? As long as you begin to feel your feelings, you're on the right track. We can't tell someone how to express their feelings. That's each person's prerogative, and there's no right or wrong way to do it.

Music

Using music as a tool to get in touch with feelings can be powerful. I don't know about you, but I listen to lots of different types of music. And depending on what I'm doing and how I'm feeling, I put on different types. When I'm going to the gym, I listen to one type of music. When I'm driving, another. When I'm sad, I have certain artists I listen to. When beginning your emotional journey, become aware of how you can use music to better understand your feelings.

Journaling

Journaling is such a powerful tool for getting in touch with the emotional self. I recently found a duffle bag filled with all my old journals from when I first got sober. Everything went into those notebooks. It's one of the reasons I'm here—I learned how to journal and discover my feelings. Charlie, my therapist, made me do it. I was resistant at first. I said, "Dude, journaling is for girls, I'm not doing it." He replied, "No, journaling is for people who want to get better, and you want to get better. So, you're going to journal every day. For two weeks. I don't care what you write or how much you write, but you're going to write every day for two weeks."

That night, I got an old notebook and sat staring at the blank paper for ten minutes. I finally wrote, "I don't know what to write." Done. He told me it didn't matter how much I wrote. The second day? "I still don't know what to write." Third day: "I still don't know what to write, and I'm really pissed off at Charlie for making me do this." Finally, on the fourth day, stuff just started to come out and I was writing *pages* a day. It helped so much.

One time, I wrote a story about a green-haired boy born into a blue-haired world, how he always felt out of place and never belonged. One day, he found a room full of other green-haired people and felt better. Writing stories helped me deal with the feelings I was having. I was in so much pain back then, but the funny thing is, in re-reading them now I can't even remember some of the events or breakups that once hurt so much. I found that time does heal all wounds.

"You cannot be lonely if you like the person you're alone with." ~Wayne Dyer

Acknowledge Every Feeling

It's time to get back to what our feelings really are and be okay with every one of them. Feelings are like a rainbow. You can't have one color without having all the others. There's no such thing as good feelings or bad feelings; feelings just *are* and it's important to realize that.

When I give my feelings too much power, however, they start to control me. If I give my fear power, then my fear starts to control me. Think of fear like this: False Evidence Appearing Real. Many times, I become fearful of things that I roll around in my head until they just get bigger. I begin to create "worst case scenarios" and start "what if-ing." The fear gains strength and momentum to the point where it's difficult to see anything else. By journaling, talking to friends and professionals, I can put the fear back in perspective and see what is really going on.

If I give my anger power, then my anger starts to control me. Same with my other feelings. If I just let my feelings be what they are and let them flow like a river, then they start to work themselves out.

Again, write in a journal or find someone that you can trust and talk to them about how you are feeling. Share your anger, talk about your sadness, talk about your hurt, talk to them about your happiness.

I find that we even stuff our happiness. Something exciting and fun happens in our life, and we're afraid that if we go to someone and say, "Wow! I just aced that test and I feel like I want to dance," we are concerned other people would look at us strangely. If we just started jumping up and down and dancing around, we fear that people would say, "Boy, what's wrong with you?" So, we're not even allowed to have our happiness.

Likewise, we feel we are not allowed to acknowledge our accomplishments. If I do a presentation and it goes really well and I say, "Wow, I really did a great job!" I might think people are going to say, "Jeez, what an ego you have." But is that really ego or is it confidence? Isn't it okay for me to acknowledge my successes? I think it is time to acknowledge the things we do well and be okay with it. Our society teaches us that's it's not okay, but I'm here to say it is healthy and it's necessary.

"Confront the dark parts of yourself, and work to banish them with illumination and forgiveness. Your willingness to wrestle with your demons will cause your angels to sing." ~August Wilson

Get to Know Your Feelings

To nourish and exercise our emotional selves, the key is to identify our feelings. In other words, start to practice feeling your feelings.

When I first started doing exploring my emotional self, I pictured all of my feelings being little kids running around and each one had a name. One was fear, one was sadness, one was anger, one was hurt. What I pictured myself doing was going to each of these little kids and talking to them and getting to know them.

I'd go to my fear, who was cowering in the corner and slowly approach. I'd say, "Hey, come out here, it will be alright now, talk to me." In learning how to talk to my fear and get to know my fear, I actually become less frightened. I turned around and there was my anger. This little boy, this little ball of anger was just hitting his head on the wall. He was so angry. I went up to him and said, "Hey, what's going on?" I started talking to him about his anger and finding out which parts of it came from fear and which from hurt.

When you take a look at your anger and try to break it down, it helps to take an honest look at it. Think about the last time you got angry, truly angry about something. At its core, was it a hurt, or was it a fear? Was it something or someone that hurt your feelings, or was it something that you were afraid of? Most of the time anger comes from a fear of not getting something t you want, or a fear of losing something you have. Probably about ninety percent of the time, these are the reasons we feel angry.

I was looking around and got to know my hurt, my frustration, and my elation. I stumbled upon my happiness. I got to know my happiness and I love my happiness. I love my fear today, I love my anger. My anger can be so refreshing, but I don't use my anger against anyone else. Today, my anger doesn't hurt me and my anger doesn't hurt other people. I've learned how to be okay with my anger, to acknowledge it and let it out in healthy ways.

"If you cannot find peace within yourself, you will never find it anywhere else." ~Marvin Gaye

Use Your Rake

When we deny, hide, or try to stuff a feeling, it doesn't just magically go away. One of my least favorite inventions is the leaf blower, because after you use it, the leaves are still there. The dirt and debris were just moved somewhere else. That's what feelings are like— you gotta get your rake, not just try to blow them to the side, then pretend they aren't there anymore.

As I was looking to get in touch with my emotional self many years ago, it was like opening a door to a room that was knee-deep in trash. And not just any trash. It was old, smelly, decomposing trash that had been there for years! Every time I opened the door, it would smell so bad that I didn't want to go anywhere near it. So, I just closed it. But the smell lingered, and it was nasty. Feelings leak out all over the place when I least want them to.

One day, I decided *I'm just going to go clean up the trash.* I said, "Okay, what's my tool? A teaspoon?" *Great.* Little by little, I started to get rid of the garbage. What I found after a while was a little shovel. My tools improved. Then, "Whoa, a bigger shovel!" I was dealing with my junk and getting better at doing so along the way.

Later on, I was in the room doing my cleaning, and I found something. I wiped it off and saw something really beautiful about myself that I didn't even know existed, because it was covered up under all that garbage. This beautiful thing I found was my ability to speak to people. Then I found my empathy, my compassion, and my desire to be of service. All these treasures were buried in the trash. When I cleaned them off, it was this amazing sense of: "Look what I found!"

Is there still trash in my room right now? Yes! Trash happens. But it's about working on it and getting rid of it—not trying to stick it some place or try to hide it or spray perfume on it. Today my "room" is no longer knee deep in trash. Today, I can see the floor!

Quick Tips and Ideas for Nourishing and Exercising Your Emotional Self:

- Listen to music
- Watch nature
- Talk to friends
- Go to therapy
- Be of service
- Be observant of others and their feelings
- Make eye contact with those who seem safe and smile
- Journal: write down your feelings, then a time in your life when you experienced them
- Become aware of what triggers each of your feelings and feel them when they come up
- Get to know your feelings, introduce yourself to each of them
- Picture yourself as a child experiencing each feeling. Go to that child in your mind and talk to them. Tell her or him that it's okay to have that feeling. Too many times parents tell kids, "Don't be sad." Or, "Don't be scared." All that does is confuse the child, because to them the feeling is real. It's time to wake up those feelings and get to know them for what they are.
- Feelings are better when embraced and not hidden or ignored

94

Chapter 12: Spiritual Self

"You yourself, as much as anybody in the entire universe, deserve your love and affection."
~Sharon Salzberg

I love discussing the spiritual part of self. But one thing I want to stipulate right now is to me, there is a difference between spirituality and religion—a big difference. I know that there are some people out there who find their spirituality through their religion and I think that's great. If you're someone who can do this, more power to you. That said, I've worked with a lot of people who have a tough time with the religion versus spirituality thing. Here's why: Think about someone you know who calls themselves very religious, but is not very spiritual at all. Yeah, you can probably think of a few of those people.

Now, think of some people you know who are very spiritual, but not very religious. There are some of those too, right? So, these two concepts are not synonymous; they can be separated.

Religion is something created by others that we take into ourselves (outside → in); spirituality is something that we create within ourselves that we take to others (inside → out). To me, God or Source, or Higher Power, or whatever you choose to call Her or Him is found within you, not outside of yourself.

When I talk about God, I'm not talking about the guy sitting in the heavens with the white beard, the white robes and the scorecard. That's not the kind of God I'm talking about at all. A Native American speaker I heard one time spoke about the fact that there is only one light, but many lampshades. I like that; this idea made a lot of sense to me. So, what I'm talking about here is that Light source. You can put whatever shade is most appealing to you on the source.

Note: When I talk about this concept in the rest of this chapter, I will be referring to the Source as "God" in the male form, just to simplify things.

"Treasure the magnificent being that you are and recognize first and foremost you're not here as a human being only. You're a spiritual being having a human experience." ~Wayne Dyer

The Outlet in the Wall

The God concept is kind of like an outlet in the wall. On its own, the outlet does nothing at all. It just sits there. But once you find it and plug into it, you have all the energy you need.

Learning how to tap into that energy source and learning how to nourish and exercise this aspect of self is so important. Fortunately, there are so many ways to do it—prayer, meditation, going to church, synagogue, or mosque, reading the Bible, Torah, or other spiritual materials, watching the sunset, taking a walk, listening to music.

To me, watching the sunset is one of the most spiritual things we can do. Actually, anything that connects us to nature has a very spiritual component to it.

When we talk about religion and spirituality, I want to reiterate the fact that everyone needs to do what works for *them*. Remember when I was talking about the physical self, and the idea that if I'm a runner and you're a swimmer, then you're not really doing it right? This attitude sounds ridiculous when we put it in these terms, but how many people do we know who do this with religion? "Well, I'm religion A so I found God, but you are religion B so you're doing it the wrong way." To me, this is just as ridiculous. I believe that God is so powerful that if He wanted us to have only one way to find Him, we would only have one religion. Instead, He wants us to find Him in whatever way is best for us. There's no right way or wrong way to find God, as long as you do, in whatever form works for you.

Defining someone by their religion is as ridiculous as saying, "Wait, you eat Cheerios? That's not cereal. You're going to starve to death. I eat Raisin Bran. That's the only *real* cereal. All my friends and family know that. We have been eating Raisin Bran for generations and if you don't eat Raisin Bran like we do, you're not eating cereal. In fact, they should take those other fakes off of the cereal shelf and only have Raisin Bran. Then the world would be a better place." *Really?*

Everyone gets to nourish their spiritual selves on their own terms, using the practices, habits, or traditions that work for them.

> *"The journey is what brings us happiness, not the destination." ~Dan Millman, Way of the Peaceful Warrior: A Book That Changes Lives*

A Greater Force

When I first got sober, I had a therapist who helped me tremendously, and people would just come out of the woodwork to assist and help and support. I realized then, there's a greater force out there. When I learned how to tap into it, that's when my spiritual self started to come alive.

My spirituality isn't really rooted in any particular doctrine. I was raised Jewish, but I think Jesus had some great things to say. Muhammad was very spiritual. Again, there's no "right" or "wrong" way to tap into your spiritual self. Spirituality comes from everywhere. One of the things I really like about the 12-step programs is when they talk about a Higher Power, it doesn't have to be God. It's just a power greater than you. One of my mentors said, "Can you create a tree?" My answer was "no." Okay, so, nature is a power greater than you. Can you go down to the beach and stop a wave? No. So, the ocean is a power greater than you. It was here long before you were here, and it'll be here long after you're gone. These are powers greater than you.

When I was three weeks sober, I went to see my rabbi. I said, "I'm in this 12-step program, I'm an addict." Now, this is a man who was probably about 60 at that time. He escaped the Nazis in WWII. He and his brother were hiding in a shack, and they were starving. So, they said, "We need to go find food."

His brother took one road, he took another. They left and were about a hundred yards out, and the Nazis caught his brother and killed him. He saw it happen, and he bolted. When he survived the war, he decided to help others and become a rabbi. He said to me, "I don't know anything about addiction. But for now, you need to find God and a higher power. You can put God on a shelf if you like. He'll be there when you need him. But look inside of yourself; there are two parts to who you are.

"There's part of you that hurts people and yourself and is destructive and does drugs. But there's this other part of you who is kind, loving, and wants to do well in the world. For a long time, the first one has been the higher power inside of you. It's time to make the second your higher power."

So, whenever I would step into a situation, I would think, "What can I do to be kind and loving right now?" Instead of, "Hmm, what's in this for me?" When I started to do that, I noticed amazing things were happening in my life. Job offers came out of nowhere and I got back into school. Many things started to work out in my life in a very positive way.

"Somewhere within us all, there does exist a supreme self who is eternally at peace." ~Elizabeth Gilbert, Eat Pray Love

Here's an example of how things started to turn around for me: I got expelled from San Diego State twice in my active addiction days. In order to get back in, the Assistant Dean of the College of Sciences said, "You need to take one class, Experimental Psychology. Get a C or better and I'll let you back into the school." I looked at the catalogue, there were about eight sections of experimental psych. I didn't know which one to pick, so I went for Tuesday and Thursday at 11:00. I didn't want to go too early, I guess, and two days a week instead of three sounded better. I went to the first day of class, and afterward went up to the professor and said, "Hi, my name is Randy, I need to get a C or better in this class and I'm willing to do whatever it takes to make that happen. I'm in recovery from addiction and I'm looking to get my life back together." She said, "Why did you choose this section? I've been in Al-Anon for 25 years. I'm not going to enable you, but I am going to help you. I'll make sure you get your C or better."

Those kinds of things happen to me all the time. When I clicked into this practice of building my self-esteem and tapping into the four parts of self and nourishing and exercising, great things began to happen. Oh, and I did get a C in the class.

Magic Moments

Years ago, my wife came to me and said, "Oh no, we need $6,200 in order to make our budget this month." I replied, "Wow, how did it get to be so much? Okay, let's just see what happens." That day, she went to the mailbox and found a consulting check that I forgot I even had coming. Guess how much it was for? $6,200!

To me, that's the Universe's way of saying, "I've got you. You're on the right track."

God doesn't say, "Randy, I want you to go to the right." We don't usually get clear directions like that. So, we have to watch for the signs that tell us we're on the right path. That's why when someone gives me too much change at a cashier's window, I immediately say, "Oh, you gave me too much change." Keep your karma flow going in the right direction. Do the right thing when given an opportunity. Karma, life, source, light...when you're clicking with it, good things just happen.

I first started noticing these kinds of magic moments early on in my recovery, when I started living a more spiritual life and tapping into that energy source. When I finally did connect, that's when I started to notice the really cool stuff. Gratitude is the key. Gratitude and humility.

"Doubt is a pain too lonely to know that faith is his twin brother." ~*Kahlil Gibran*

Quick Tips and Ideas for Nourishing Your Spiritual Self:

- Prayer
- Meditation
- Read the Bible, Torah, Koran or other spiritual texts
- Go to church, temple, mosque, or better yet, attend a service from a faith different from your own
- Listen to music
- Be of service
- Find gratitude for things in your life
- Become aware of the awesomeness of nature (ocean, trees, lakes, etc.)
- Accept others for having a different path to Source than you do

Chapter 13: Nourishing All Four

"Everything that happens to you is a reflection of what you believe about yourself. We cannot outperform our level of self-esteem." ~Iyanla Vanzant

What you're probably noticing is there are some activities we've mentioned that can nourish more than one part of self. I know for some people, running is very meditative and very spiritual. Mentally, it's very clearing. Just the mere fact of going out for a run can exercise and nourish the physical self, the mental self, and the spiritual self. For some people, it nourishes the emotional self, too.

Find things that work for you and stick with them. Likewise, we need to give people the right to choose their own path, whatever that path is, even if it's different from ours.

Honor All Parts of Yourself

Each aspect of self is a quarter of who you are. If you're not dealing with one part of self, the best you

105

can do in life is 75%, a C. Not dealing with two parts of self in a healthy way brings this number down to 50%, an F *at your best!* And that's if you really are attending to the physical and spiritual. When you look at it this way, it's easy to see why we have so many problems and issues in our society. People are not taking care of themselves.

We need to wake people up.

As adults, we get locked in to our identities, and a lot of times these identities are completely lopsided. Here's an example of what I mean:

I work with college athletes, and when they're injured, alcohol abuse tends to go up and self-esteem goes down, because their entire *being* is dependent on an external thing—how many yards per carry, or how many points they're able to score per game. I remind them, "That's what you *do,* that is not who you *are.*" They've been reinforced with one idea their whole life: "You are your points per game." When they get an injury, it's, "Who am I now?" There are a thousand different ways to answer that question, but none of them needs to have anything to do with what goes on during a game. My favorite example of this is Dwayne Johnson, "The Rock." He talks about being a college athlete, destined to go to the NFL. But then he got injured and his career was over. He went into a huge depression and thought his life had no meaning. We know now, of course, that because of his injury, he found a different career path. And I think it worked out okay for him.

"When you dance, your purpose is not to get to a certain place on the floor. It's to enjoy each step along the way." ~Wayne Dyer

The Energy Ball

Picture your energy as a ball inside of you. Sometimes our energy ball is as big as a beach ball and sometimes it's as small as a marble. My belief is that depending on how we nourish and exercise the four parts of self, we either have the beach ball or the marble, and we're in control of that. Many times, we give our power away to other people, places, and things, but the bottom line is that we are in control of our energy ball and where our energy goes.

Depending on how we treat ourselves, that's how big or small our energy ball is going to be. It's important to be conscious of this. Whenever I get up to do one of my programs or one of my workshops, it's important for me to be conscious of having a large energy ball because I put a lot of energy into my presentations.

I watch a lot of people who fall short of taking good care of themselves. They start out with the marble energy ball and they still have to expend a lot of energy that they don't really have to begin with. They are overly stressed and can't sleep and stop eating well. They become more irritable, short tempered, and more easily frustrated. It becomes a vicious cycle. People who are working on dwindling energy reserves tend to do two things: suck up other people's energy to survive, or engage in self-destructive behaviors. They're depleted down to the core, and unfortunately, they can feel stuck. But this just isn't true. Change is difficult, but it is possible.

A Self-Esteem Depleted Society

The whole idea around work ethic in our culture tends to be about the *quantity* of work someone does, rather than the *quality* of work. If you can create the same quality of work in 30 hours as opposed to in 60, do 30! But a lot people find their worth through their work—they believe that the more they're working, the better off they are and hence the more worth they have. It's not true; I'd like you to question this assumption.

Break that cycle. Start treating yourself with dignity and respect by making more time for yourself and less at work. No one was ever on their deathbed saying, "I wish I would have spent more time in the office." Start enhancing your energy ball by making more time for yourself and those people who are important to you.

Energy Vampires

There are some people out there who just suck our energy dry. How many times have you been around someone who has had the same problem over and over for the past six months, and they aren't doing anything about it, and they just keep complaining? They're living in the problem rather than living in the solution, and they keep talking about the same thing over and over. They say, "Can I just talk to you one more time about this?" You talk to them for about a half an hour, and afterwards you feel drained. You just have no energy left at all, but *they* feel so much better.

Now *they're* energized, now *they* are motivated, now they are ready to go on with their life. What happened here is they sank their teeth into your energy ball and sucked the energy right out of you and into them. Now all of your energy is theirs and you just allowed this to happen.

Boundaries

A large part of self-esteem is establishing boundaries and being able to say no to people. Being able to say, "I love you dearly, but you've been working on this issue for six months. I don't see you doing much about it. I want to support you and I want to help you, but you need to help yourself first."

Boundaries are *so* important. I think we live in a co-dependent society where people are taught they have to give, give, give. There are times when it's okay to say, "You know, my energy is a bit too low to give you my full attention right now. Can we talk about this later?" and that has to be alright. And yes, it's hard to do.

Challenge Yourself

When my daughter was small, we were on the playground. One of the pieces of play equipment was designed to let the little kids climb these blocks, about four feet high, walk across, and then climb down.

My daughter was probably three or four years old and started climbing up. At the top, she lost her footing and fell into the sand. It was like slow motion as I watched it happen, unable to do anything to prevent the fall. Afterward, I could tell nothing was broken, but she started crying. I knew she was just scared, so I held her for a little while. Finally, she calmed down and said, "Daddy, I want to do it again."

Saying "okay," was *so hard,* because it would've been really easy for me to say, "No, let's wait until you're a little older." But I said "okay," and watched her determination. She climbed up and was very focused. There could've been a marching band behind her and she would not have blinked. She climbed up, went across and climbed back down, "Daddy, I did it!" We were both just beaming.

It would've been difficult for a lot of parents to let their little ones climb up that second time. It was difficult for me! But because of this kind of thing, my daughter has confidence in herself. A couple months ago, we took her to a Youth Group meeting that she had never been to before. When we started walking into the building, she said, "You don't have to go in with me, I'm okay. I'll see you guys when it's over." Then, she just walked right into the room filled with complete strangers. I was so proud of her.

It's important to take risks. Being complacent brings the illusion of being "safe," but does it really bring joy and happiness. Sometimes we need to fall and learn from our experiences.

I could go into all the failures I've had in my life. In school, in business, all the times I've been fired from jobs. I had this phenomenal business years ago, and it just crumbled. I chose the wrong people to lead it, I left people in positions too long. Looking back, I needed to be a harsher businessperson. But if I had been, and I was still running that business this book most likely wouldn't exist. Everything happens the way it's supposed to.

> *"You miss 100% of the shots you never take."*
> *~Wayne Gretzky*

Faith vs. Fear

Life supports us in whatever it is we want to do when we clear the obstacles. Even though it's difficult, scary, even terrifying, when we make choices guided by faith, things tend to work out. Maybe not always with the timing we prefer and sometimes the answer is no, but in the long run, everything works out when we have faith. I actually think that all prayers are answered. But the answer can be yes, no, or not yet. I love the Indiana Jones movie where he has to face the three trials. On the second one, he has to take the Leap of Faith. He comes to a huge chasm that he has to walk across. It's not until he takes the first step that he realizes there's a bridge there and he safely walks across.

I also think about the story of the Israelites crossing the Red Sea. It's not like the movie, where Moses parted the water from the safety of the shore. No, someone had to take the risk of walking into the sea until the water was up over their head, to have faith they were going to be okay. *That's* when the sea parted. It wasn't even Moses, it was someone else who volunteered.

People are afraid of so many things. Fear of failure. Fear of success. Fear of being found out. Fear of not being accepted, fear of not being liked. There are so many fears. We live in fear. I believe that fear and faith are on a balance with each other. When fear is high, faith is low. When faith is high, fear is low. It's faith in self, not just, "I believe in God." That's just one form of faith. Faith in yourself, faith in your surroundings.

All this being said, I don't want people to abruptly quit their jobs, and think "I have faith that I'll find another one." There has to be a barometer you use when you're making big decisions, to really look at all the different factors, the "How are we going to make this work?" questions. Things do need to fall into place. It's all about opening your awareness to the things that are around you, looking for opportunities. When you do this, good things happen. They just do.

When you're less in tune with reinforcing your ego, you're more present in the moment and open to opportunities to connect and even play. With ego, *it's all about me.* You're in your cocoon. Self-esteem is seeing, *I'm part of this great big world. What can I do to help?*

Raising Kids with High Self-Esteem

A lot of adults give messages to kids subconsciously. Parents don't intentionally think, "Ooh, I'm going to say this, and it's going to destroy their self-esteem." No. But because we are in such a self-esteem depleted society, kids do receive some unhelpful messages. As children learn how to navigate the world, they need to know they are loved and supported, but it's difficult with the messages they receive through the media, at school, and at home.

Ask a kindergarten class, "Who knows how to paint?" and every hand goes up in the air. Ask a middle school class, "Who knows how to paint?" Maybe you get one or two hands going timidly in the air. So, what happens in that very short seven-year period of time? What makes them doubt their ability and become so self-conscious? If *I* am asked if I can paint, my answer is, "Yes! I can paint the same stick figures today that I drew in kindergarten." My artwork most likely won't be in a museum, but I can paint!

I get asked all the time, "What can I do as a parent to raise the self-esteem of my child?" And my answer is always the same: Raise your own. When a parent starts working on their self-esteem, it has a great ripple effect in the family. Celebrate successes, don't just focus on the negative. Point out that a 95% on a test means 95% right, not just 5% wrong. It's important to build kids up, to call attention to the things they're doing right as well as the things they need to improve on.

One current issue with kids and self-esteem is the notion that we have to praise kids at all levels of participation. We give the kid a ribbon for 9th place in a race or we don't keep score at a game because we don't want to hurt anyone's feelings. I don't agree with this method of building self-esteem. In fact, I think this does more damage than good. In life, there are things we're good at and things we're not as good at. Sometimes we do our best and win, sometimes we do our best and lose. This is one of the main lessons of life.

We need to learn how to lose just as much as we need to learn how to win. We need to teach kids that they are not going to be the best at everything, and even for the things they are gifted in, they will not always win or be the best. Most importantly, winning the game or being the fastest is a skill they have, but it does not determine their level of self-esteem. The self-esteem piece comes in when they participate and do their best, not if they win or lose. Self-esteem is about the process, not the result.

"Be more concerned with your character than your reputation, because your character is what you really are, while your reputation is merely what others think you are." ~John Wooden

Building Self-Esteem in Adolescence and Beyond

Sixth to tenth grade is vital for building self-esteem. If you can help your children build it then, when they get to college or the working world, they're solid with who they are and where they fit, regardless of whether they know what they're going to do next or not.

Young adulthood, just after high school graduation, is another great time to build self-esteem. For years I was a therapist on college campuses, and students would often come in very distressed about what to do with their lives; which major to choose, what classes to take. I heard a lot of, "I *have to* be a lawyer." "What do you mean?" I'd ask. The answer was often some version of, "My dad's a lawyer, my mom's a lawyer; they expect me to be a lawyer." "Okay, what do *you* want to do?" I would ask them. "I want to be an artist." Helping these students to get in touch with Self is so important during this life stage. If we can help people find who they are, and find their niche, we'll be much better off as a society.

Someone can start this process of tuning in to that inner voice at any time of life. You have this information—these tools—*today*. It doesn't matter if you didn't build your self-esteem yesterday. Focus on the now. What little change are you going to make today that's going to help raise your self-esteem, and open new doors and new perspectives? You'll begin to notice your friends and your kids start to pick up on this new energy that you have.

I think our society would be much better off if people started to take more risks. Sure, be a lawyer during the day if that's what you really want to do, but pick up a couple of gigs performing music on the side—or whatever it is that's calling you.

"The best time to plant a tree was 20 years ago. The second best time is now." ~Chinese proverb

Balance and Perfection

To build self-esteem, it's important to be balanced. It's like a mobile. Have you ever seen a mobile hanging from the ceiling? When one part moves they all move, and when one is out of balance it throws the entire thing out of balance. Self-esteem is like that. It's time to start adjusting those little parts so we can be the best that we can be.

Keep in mind, as you work on yourself, that perfection is an illusion. It does not exist; it's always out of reach. The imperfect is perfect. One of my favorite movies is *The Last Samurai*. At one point, Tom Cruise's character is talking to the Japanese lord of the village, who is a poet. The poet says, "One of the goals of my life is to find the perfect cherry blossom."

At the end, as the poet is dying, he says, "Now I see...they're *all* perfect."

Altruism and Giving Back

Most of the people I know who have high self-esteem do some kind of service. That's such an important part of this process, because service gets you out of self. Ego is all about self; self-esteem is selfless. Part of my morning prayer every day is, "Help me be of service to others today." Sometimes it's as small as being at Epcot and taking a photo for a family so they can all be in it together. And sometimes it's much bigger than that, like volunteering to do a presentation at no cost for an organization that helps children.

Being of service is good spiritually, mentally and emotionally. And depending on what you're doing— for example, if it's something like Habitat for Humanity—it's good for your physical self as well. There are so many habits and practices that have crossover. The key is to find those things you can do once a day that nourish all four aspects of self. Service, altruism and giving back definitely fit into this category.

Ask for Support

It's hard to start building genuine self-esteem on our own. It's really important to get support, yet our society tells us we're supposed to just suck it up and do it alone. It doesn't work that way. I know there's no way I would be where I am if it wasn't for the help and support of other people.

When you take a look at situations in your life, I'm sure you'd say that when you were at your toughest times, looking for the support and aid of others is what helped bring you through. There's nothing wrong with asking for help. It's humbling, *very* humbling, but there's a difference between it being humbling and it being humiliating. Again, humiliating is the way of the ego. Humility is something that our self-esteem can handle.

Who Will You Feed?

When you're aligned with your purpose in life, all four aspects of the self will benefit. Physically, you feel excited, and have more energy. Mentally, it's like you're stimulated and ready to go. Emotionally, you feel fulfilled and spiritually, you're dialed in, thinking, "I'm doing what I'm supposed to be doing." The best self-esteem builders are the ones that tap into multiple parts of self.

When you can find something that stimulates all four, *awesome.* When I go to my kickboxing gym to work out, I'm exercising all four parts of self. Then, I get to look in the mirror the next day and see that my hard work is paying off. Sure, let's be honest, there is a little ego there when I see the cut of my deltoid muscle, but the self-esteem payoff is so much greater knowing I'm doing something really healthy for myself. Both ego and self-esteem are present in most situations, but it's like the Cherokee story of the white wolf and the black wolf. A young boy says to his grandfather, "I keep having a dream of a white wolf and a black wolf fighting. It seems to go on all night long." Ah, the grandfather replies. "The white wolf represents love, faith, gratitude, forgiveness, patience, peace and hope. The black wolf is hatred, rage, cruelty, fear, intolerance and ego."

"Oh," the boy says. "Well, which one will win the fight?"

The wise grandfather replies, "The one you feed."

Which one do you want to feed? Do you want to feed your ego, or feed your self-esteem? It's your decision, every single day.

Conclusion

"The journey of a thousand miles begins with one step." ~Lao Tzu

Now, it's up to you. Self-esteem is not the kind of thing you can go to the store and purchase for $1.99. This is not something anyone can give you.

To illustrate this journey that we're on in building self-esteem, and this journey in life, I'd like to tell you the story of the Road to Hana. Hana is this little town on the island of Maui in Hawaii. What people hear when they go to Maui is, "You have to go to Hana." So, these tourists get in their rental car and they go to Hana.

The Road to Hana is about 50 miles long and it takes about two hours to get there because the road is about one and a half lanes wide for two-way traffic. On one side of the road is a two-hundred-foot cliff down to the water, and on the other side is a jungle. While you're going around these hairpin turns there are vans and other cars whipping by you going the other way. It can be pretty dangerous unless you go the recommended 15 or 20 miles an hour, but a lot of tourists don't want to do that, they want to get to Hana! So, they risk their lives and they zip around these corners and they finally get to Hana.

And when they get to Hana, there's not much there.

Basically, there's a gas station, a little general store where you can buy a T-shirt that says *I survived the Road to Hana* and a hotel that has about 12 rooms. Sure, you can see the Seven Sacred Pools, which is really beautiful, but a lot of times, the tourists get to Hana and they're so frustrated. They say, "That's it?! I wasted a day of my vacation and nearly killed myself getting here and all I get is a sandwich and a t-shirt?!" Why? Because they were in such a big hurry to get *there* that they didn't notice the road along the way. Then, all the way back, the entire two hours, all they can do is complain about how horrible Hana was and that they just wasted a day of their vacation.

Now, here's the other side of the story. There are those of us who have been to Hana that know that the Road to Hana is one of the most beautiful roads in the entire world. Every time you turn one of those corners, you have a 200-foot view down to the ocean, and it is blue like you have never seen blue before. The waves are crashing on the beach, and sometimes you can see whales or dolphins playing in the water. It is so beautiful and so serene. Then, on the other side when you look up into the jungle, it is so green, so beautiful. Sometimes you can see waterfalls coming down, and the birds are so many different colors; it is just the most gorgeous, picturesque scene you'd ever want to see.

You get to Hana and have something to eat at the general store and fill up your gas tank and maybe go over to the pools and hang out for a while. You talk about how beautiful the Road was and appreciate the fact that you just enjoyed one of the most beautiful drives in the world. On the way back, you get to see it all over again.

I love the Road to Hana. Not only is traveling it one of my favorite things to do, but it is a great illustration of how life works. Too many times, we feel compelled to get "there" that we forget to enjoy the journey along the way.

"Nobody can go back and start a new beginning, but anyone can start today and make a new ending."
~Maria Robinson

The Turtle

Similarly, and one of my all-time favorite stories to tell, is about the time I was scuba diving in Hawaii. I love diving! I'm a Pisces, so when I get in the water, I'm at home. On this particular day, the water was flat, like glass. The dive master was so psyched. He said, "Listen, we only get conditions like this about three or four times a year, so we get to go to a dive site we don't normally get to go to. So, we're going to a site called Turtle Town."

The visibility was crazy, it was like swimming in an aquarium. The dive master told us to find a dive buddy and look for turtles. I got in the water and it was warm, and we had 200-foot visibility. It was the most amazing dive I'd ever been on. There were turtles *everywhere*. All of a sudden, I saw a big grandfather of a turtle perched in the sand. It was so beautiful, and he was just sitting there, almost like he was meditating. I moved up to him and he started swimming, checking me out with his big black eyes. I swam parallel to him. He didn't swim away from me, he didn't swim faster, he just started swimming. I was swimming next to him for a while, then I reached over and started petting his shell. What I didn't know then, but I do know now, is touching a Hawaiian sea turtle is illegal, with a fine and jail time. But again, I didn't know that.

126

I was petting his shell and he didn't go anywhere, we just kept swimming together. Then I swam up over his back and hung on to his shell and we started cruising along together. I was riding a turtle! To this day, it was one of the most exciting experiences in my entire life, swimming with that turtle. I was kicking a little, but he was doing most of the work (or *she* was doing most of the work, I'm not really sure). After a while, I had the thought, "Woah, wait a minute. How long have I been with the turtle? Where's my dive buddy? How deep are we? Where's the boat!?" Have you ever had an experience where you were so into the moment you lost track of everything else? Yeah, well that's not a good thing when you're scuba diving. I looked over each shoulder and my dive buddy was nowhere to be seen. I thought, "Oh great, my dive buddy is now this turtle." I looked up and saw that we were about 30-40 feet underwater so I knew I was safe and could get to the surface if I ran out of air. Then I thought, "Which way is the boat?" After an assessment of which way we were swimming and where I remembered the boat being, I realized we were swimming away from the boat! And it was probably pretty far away.

I didn't feel like swimming that far so I came up with a brilliant idea. I'll just turn the turtle around and he can take me back to the boat. Then I had the follow up thought, "Wait until they get a load of me, riding on the back of a turtle. How cool am I going to look?!"

Of course, this meant I was letting ego get in the way of this wonderful experience. I gently nudged his shell to the right, thinking he would turn to the right. Then my thought was, when he turned all the way around I'll straighten him out and we'll go back to the boat. Well, it didn't quite work out that way. As I tried to turn him right, he just suddenly bolted and took off to the left. There was nothing I could do stop him.

What I realized at that moment was that he *let* me ride him. He *allowed* me to have that experience because he could have taken off at any time. But, as soon as I tried to control the situation, as soon as I tried to exert ego (let him do the work and wait until they get a load of me), he was gone. I learned a lot from that experience.

Trying to control things is not always the best way to go. Sometimes it is better to just let things be what they are rather than trying to fix them or make a situation better or make it different than what it actually is. So, the main lesson here is "Don't turn the turtle!" Enjoy all the gifts that life gives you, even if they seem few and far between.

I wish you the best on your journey. I wish you health, I wish you happiness and I wish you all the success you allow yourself to have.

Workbook

Part 1

Where are you on the continuum?

Ego |--| Self-Esteem

Draw an X to represent where you are as you start this process. Once a month, (set a reminder on your calendar) look again and see what kind of progress you've made.

Part 2

Obstacles

Step 1. What are your obstacle words and phrases? List them all and rank the top three.

Step 2. Start becoming more aware of how often you use them and in what context.

Step 3. Determine the underlying motive for your obstacle words (fear, control, etc.).

Step 4. Check in once a month to see if you're using your obstacle words less often. Ask a trusted friend or partner to help you identify when you use them.

Part 3

Building Self-Esteem: Four Parts of Self

Look at what you can do to exercise and nourish the four parts of self. List what you're going to do for each part. I suggest journaling become a part of your daily or weekly routine for mental and emotional health.

Physical:

Mental:

Emotional:

Spiritual:

About Randy

An empathic warrior who has overcome many obstacles, Randy isn't afraid to get in the trenches with his readers. He'll help you identify—and dig yourself out from—the things keeping you buried or struggling. Randy's years as a therapist, university administrator, and health promotion expert are grounded in his own journey of personal growth. Randy is a survivor—a survivor of addiction, of self-hatred, and of our often toxic, ego-soaked culture.

Today, Randy is a speaker who helps audiences around the country and the world find their paths in life and learn the self-esteem building skills necessary to be positive, productive, and fulfilled members of society. He has provided memorable keynotes and paradigm-shifting leadership workshops at schools including Notre Dame, Brown, Johns Hopkins and Valencia Community College, among many others. Randy is now dedicating his life to his true passion and helping others to do the same.

Learn more at www.theriseorg.com.